Another Day Another Sunset

Another Day Another Sunset

Hannah Stogner

LPH

LUMINARY PUBLISHING HOUSE

For permissions, licensing, or usage inquiries, please contact: Luminary Publishing House, LLC at inquire@luminarypublishinghouse.com

ISBN (Paperback):978-1-968972-16-5

ISBN (Hardcover):978-1-968972-17-2

Cover design by Julsiji http://julsiji.wordpress.com/

LUMINARY PUBLISHING HOUSE

Sincerely, Me

Dear 2021 me,

A lot has changed

We are no longer the same

We know better now and don't feel

shame for the things we never

claimed but somehow

still took the blame for.

I am no longer you.

You are no longer me.

I used to grieve your absence.

I used to think it was tragic.

I've broken a lot of your habits.

And now I am no longer saddened.

Sincerely, Me

Forgetting

People say forgetting is always the hardest thing to do.

And it is.

But focusing on trying to forget

keeps the memory in its place.

Leaving you to always feel that unrest.

Until life sweeps you up in its tide,

giving your mind

the time to do what you always wanted.

And by then, one day you'll think.

What was I trying to forget?

Lie In A Field Of Flowers

Peaceful, quiet, serene.

A field of flowers covers me.

A breath of sweet aroma

and a sight of soft petals.

A grass bed to doze upon

a field of sunlight and sweet daisies.

People Are Like Stones In My Pocket

People are like stones.

Weighing you down till you can barely take another step.

Till your pockets start to rip.

Till you start to trip,

against their weight

and you can't escape.

Cold And Warm

Cold and warm.

Two opposites.

One, I welcome on a daily basis.

The other only on rare occasions.

Warmth, a feeling I seek late at night.

Cold, a feeling I shrink from.

Early in the sunrise, layered with cold

I run away from it into the arms of warmth.

The scale is forever unbalanced.

Still, I wake with both beside me.

And both live within me, dancing in quiet war.

Mom

My mom is the most beautiful woman alive.

She's my favorite person.

She's one of a kind.

My mom is my best friend, my caretaker, my motivation.

She's my reason to be great.

I will love her all the way to Neverland.

My mom is my reason for getting up every morning.

My reason for loving so hard.

Everything I do is for her, my mom.

How dear you are to me.

Passenger

Passenger,

sitting in a car,

watching the world blur by.

The passenger watches quietly as the car turns down a road.

The passenger has thought about being behind the wheel,

but is held back by fear.

The passenger, who, for once, wants to be the driver.

But is too scared to take the wheel.

Coincidences

How often are coincidences really just that?

A coincidence.

How many times did you read too deeply into something insignificant?

All for the sake of saying a coincidence doesn't happen twice.

Unprepared

I was unprepared for his name to flash across my screen.

Deep down, I know what it means.

Woman will continue to bleed,

will continue to die.

We are unprepared for the challenges we'll face.

Other people will laugh in my face.

When I say his name with disgust and call him a disgrace.

He is a danger to us all, but only the ones with their eyes open can hear the warning call.

Lavender

Lavender, a smell that's sometimes so sickeningly sweet.

And other times, one that I appreciate.

A smell that sometimes brings nausea and other times cures stress and headaches.

Oh, lavender, a smell I love-hate.

It Will Pass

It will pass, the pain and suffering.

The tears and anguish.

The anger and frustration.

The apathy and desperation.

It will pass.

The numbness and indifference.

The solitude and isolation.

You never deserved it,

It will pass.

The craving for revenge,

to watch others suffer the same way you did

it will pass.

The grief will dull.

The trauma will remain.

But everything else will pass.

October

Autumn leaves in the air.

Spiraling down with a golden flair.

Crisp winds whisper through trees.

Carrying secrets on an amber breeze.

The smell of pumpkin spice lingers near,

a scent that means October's here.

Cinnamon, nutmeg, clove, and cream.

A cozy comfort, like a dream.

Time for pumpkin decorations,

carved with care and wild imaginations.

Grinning faces, candlelight glow.

Flickering softly through the window.

For scary stories and movie marathons,

under blankets till the break of dawn.

Ghost tales told in quiet hush,

while outside, the world turns cold and plush.

Sweaters worn and cocoa sipped.

Pages of mysteries gently flipped.

Porch lights flicker, candy awaits.

Little footsteps at the gates.

October brings a magic old,

In hues of orange, red, and gold.

A time of wonder, warmth, and chills,

Of haunted houses on shadowed hills.

Fleeting Warmth

Fleeting warmth,

a feeling all too familiar.

Whether it's the embrace from your mother that ends all too soon.

Or the soft sound of laughter from your friend.

It's a certain kind of warmth I wish to cling to.

One that fills me up and leaves my chest buzzing.

A fleeting warmth you wish to keep.

To keep you warm in its gentle heat.

Once Again

Once again, the world has failed me, failed us.

Never making the right decisions for the sake of appearance.

Once again, women have been hurt.

The mothers, daughters, sisters, and aunts.

Once again, we are burned.

By the sexism of the world, we bring life into.

Once again, the world fails me.

In Spite Of It All

If you had ever called me

I would have answered.

If you had ever wanted to talk it out

I would have tried to work it out.

For you, in spite of it all,

I would have put all lies and pain aside for you.

In spite of it all,

A part of me still loves you.

Strangers Again

From strangers, to friends, to lovers, to strangers again.

I can pass you by

while knowing your favorite color.

You pass me by while knowing my darkest secrets.

How can people who are strangers to each other,

know what they wanted to be when they graduated?

How can strangers have been so close but now be so far apart?

We were strangers once.

Now we are strangers again.

Sister

We look alike, and have different names.

Our dad is the same.

Grew up never knowing you were there

but you were always near.

We like the same artists.

Even wear the same glasses.

It freaks my mom out how mirrored we are.

No doubt that we're sisters.

One that I always missed,

even before I knew you were out there.

A Dying Flower Bush

Once a vibrant bush of flowers so bright

A bush that had been formed in spring's warmth and sunlight

Petals once youthful and soft

Now faded and withered

Bulbs that once promised bloom

Now lower to the ground, in dark brown, and bring gloom.

Leaves once green and nice to the eye

Now they're are full of holes and bug bites

Roots once firm and deep in the soil

Are now frail and broken, with nothing to offer

Decay now covers what once had beauty.

Running Low

Energy, most days I have none.

Tank on E

Instead of being productive, I'll roll over to bed rot.

Soft Brown Eyes

Soft brown eyes are what I have,

But to me, they're nothing but black.

People say they love my eyes,

I never understood until I looked closely at my mother's

She has soft brown eyes

Like me.

I can see the beauty in them when I look at her.

Her brown eyes are full of love and care.

I look like my mother.

I think I have her eyes.

They are no longer black and empty to me when I look in the mirror,

Now I just see my mom's soft brown eyes.

Love Loudly

I wish to love loudly.

I wish to be loved just as loud.

I want my love to be strong.

To love without doubt is what I crave.

To be loved equally every day.

I want to give out my love and get some back in return.

I want to be known by someone like I'm the back of their hand.

I want someone to love me effortlessly because I'd love them the same.

I want a love that is loud and bright.

A love that never dies.

New Beginnings

A new beginning,

I crave nothing more than a new beginning.

To be in a fresh place with all new people,

A new house, a place for me to start fresh.

To leave behind the echoes of who I was,

the rooms are heavy with old versions of me.

To wake without the weight of memory,

without familiar ghosts calling my name.

I want air that has never known my breath.

Golden Sunshine

Golden sunshine, a beauty I adore.

Something I really should stop for.

I admire it too little and need to bask in it more.

I will, oh my dear golden sunshine,

I really will try to love you more.

16

16, It's not much different from 17.

But now it feels like it's been so long since I was 16.

When, truly, it's only been 22 days.

16 I miss you.

Old Records

Sometimes I feel like an old record,

Scratched and damaged.

Repeating the same memory over and over

It's been 3 years since it all happened,

I've changed and grown.

Yet the memories play on repeat

like an old record scratching over and over and over and over.

Dancing Flames

Flames, dancing so prettily around the candle,

So soft but so dangerous.

Chipping away at the wax with every passing moment.

Flames flickering in the dark room,

providing solace with its light.

While strong enough to burn your finger.

If you get too close,

there's beauty in the danger.

There's warmth in the light of dancing flames.

The Need To Be Great

The need is deep in my bones.

Tied in the deepest parts of my DNA and soul.

The need to be successful.

The need to be great.

The need to be what I strive to be.

Fear Of Missing Out

Lately, I've been thinking about the things I could be missing.

The friends, the experiences, all for the sake of something else.

The fear of missing out is something I hold close to me,

constantly wondering if I made the right choice.

Choosing writing over teenagehood.

My biggest fear is missing out,

and it's all for nothing.

The fear of missing out and the need to be great.

Intertwining themselves inside my bodily chemistry.

Second Chances

I always believed everyone deserves a second chance.

A time to redeem themselves,

I learned that second chances are often wasted

They will always be taken for granted.

Choke On Your Words

I hope you choke on your words.

That every time you try to tell a lie,

or sew a false narrative,

that the words get stuck inside your throat.

Choke on your words for all the lies you've spread.

For all the friendships you've ended.

Choke on your lies and never utter another word.

The Grief Of Someone Who Is Not Dead

I grieve you even though you're not gone.

You haunt me in a way that I can't seem to shake.

I regard you as if you're truly dead.

I can't seem to get you out of my head.

I miss parts of you, the things I used to know so well.

Now, when I think of you,

I want you to go to hell.

I miss you even when you're not dead.

You're a ghost in my mind that I wish were gone.

Unrequited Love

Back and forth,

like waves that never touch the shore.

Never a firm answer.

Just echoes of "maybe" and "not sure."

A yes on one day,

hope rising like the morning sun.

Maybe the next,

and that hope comes undone.

Unrequited love.

It truly messes with the brain,

a cycle of longing and self-doubt.

Of silent joy followed by pain.

Strung along by feelings,

tangled like a thread in trembling hands.

Reading into every glance,

trying hard to understand.

Frustrated thoughts like static noise.

Running wild and uncontained.

Wishing for clarity,

even if it means more pain.

I'd rather be rejected.

A clean cut, sharp and clear.

Then kept on unstable footing,

chained to both hope and fear.

A heart should not be a maybe.

It deserves a yes or a goodbye.

But I linger in the in-between,

Too stubborn to let my love die.

So here I stay,

waiting on words that never come.

Writing poems to silence,

for a love that's given none.

Some Things Shatter, Some Things Bloom

Some things shatter in the cold weather.

Crack under someone's pressure.

Wither away until they are small and bitter.

Then some bloom, even in the cold weather

Because they have a warm shelter, keeping them centered

Maybe it's not the frost that decides our fate,

but what we let inside our chest.

Some hearts hold a little sun

tucked between their ribs, a quiet,

steady ember that says not yet,

when the world says freeze.

And when spring finally comes,

It doesn't make them new, just seen.

Pieces Glued Together

Broken glass, jagged and sharp.

Glued together haphazardly, still broken in parts.

Try to fill it with water and watch it seep through the cracks,

puddling at the bottom till the glass is empty.

Gluing pieces together can only go so far,

not truly fixing what's broken.

Only offering a rudimentary fix.

Until it ultimately breaks again.

Are We Still Friends?

The distance is loud, our messages empty.

We barely talk, just watching each other through a screen.

When we get to this point, are we really still friends?

I don't think we can call each other that anymore.

But yet I wonder, are we still friends in your head?

I Wish I Could Remember You Better

Sometimes I wish I could remember you better

Remember your smile, your voice, your eyes.

I wish I remembered our time together.

The memories we shared,

which are now a distant fog lost in the wind.

The memory of you is locked away in my brain.

Chained by the pain you've brought.

I wish I could remember the good days.

The ones that felt like the sun's end-of-day rays.

Bittersweet Melody

Bittersweet memories, a tragedy really

Songs used to play so beautifully,

now everything is just dead to me.

Seaside

Sand, sunlight, and salty water

Seaside beach trip

mother and brother in tow.

A family day by the sea.

Chips and sandwiches, sodas too.

More days like this, I'd appreciate.

My two favorite people and the pretty nature.

Wave after wave, birds squawking,

music playing, the umbrella swaying in the wind.

I Met My Younger Self For Coffee

She was 10 minutes early.

I was 5 minutes early.

She wore jeans she got from her nana and a sweater.

I wore jeans similar to hers but newer,

still in a sweater.

She ordered a caramel latte,

I ordered the same.

She told me she was excited for her sophomore year

of high school with her friends.

Still worrying about the same people who always gave her problems.

I told her she switched to homeschool.

And those friends she thought she was so close with,

left her at a moment's notice.

She was sad, but I comforted her.

Told her she meets better people,

a new friend that easily fills all the spots of the ones that left.

She asks what she's doing now that she's graduated.

I tell her she's chasing her dreams.

Doing something she never thought she'd have the guts to do.

That she put herself out there and is starting to see the fruits of her labor.

I tell her that she's happy.

That she is content with where she is at.

That the sadness she's felt has dulled.

That it's no longer at the forefront of her mind.

And everything she stresses over

is no longer at the forefront of her mind.

She leaves the coffee shop with a small smile

but uncertainty in her eyes.

I stay at the table, watching her leave.

Sad to watch her go, but happy to know what's ahead of her.

A

She's beautiful.

Smart.

Creative.

Determined.

All the things I could want in a girl.

She's special.

I can feel it like a missing puzzle piece I didn't know was there.

Fitting just right, in the best way.

Distance

The distance won't make a difference for me.

I'll wait through the hours for you to respond to me.

I cherish every time my phone lights up from a message sent by you.

The distance looms over us, but it seems so small every time I see your smile.

I barely know what to do.

Scotland

I yearn for a place that I've never been to.

My bones ache for it.

My heart is tied there even though my eyes have never seen it.

I know deep down, I'm meant to do great things there.

Live, love, thrive.

I yearn for the land I haven't touched.

But somewhere,

so deep inside me, I know, I will get there one day.

Nonchalant

Nonchalant, something quite frankly I am not.

I can't hide how I feel.

A byproduct of being a person that

doesn't know the meaning of giving their heart a shield.

Pictures

Whenever you send me one, it lights up my day.

Your smile shining in every single one of them.

They make my heart flutter as I smile alongside you.

You enrapture me. I could stare at your pictures for hours.

Memorizing your eyes and nose,

just staring at every part of the beauty that is you.

Never Get To Know

They don't know me.

They like to think and pretend that they do,

but they don't.

They're thinking of an old version of me.

A version they did indeed once know.

But that version is gone.

Long gone.

That me was buried the same day you left.

The me now is different.

The version you will never get to know.

They can watch me through screens,

stalk through fake accounts.

But they will never truly know this version of me.

They will never know me again.

Painter

Maybe in another life, I was a painter.

Sketching the horizons of beautiful oceans.

Using all the colors my eyes could see,

to paint mountains on a Scottish countryside.

If I were a particularly good painter,

I'd try to capture the warmth and light of your eyes.

Using every brown I found, mixing them together with just a hint of gold.

In hopes that I'd replicate the beauty that your gentle eyes hold.

I Carry The Pieces Of People I've Lost

I carry the pieces of people.

Tiny little shards.

Things they've said.

Or things they've done.

They stick to me.

They shape me and morph me over the years.

Mini lessons are taught by each person I pass and lose.

Love The Silence

I learned to love the silence.

To appreciate the moments where I could just be.

Just breathe.

There's a beauty in being alone in silence.

Resting and charging.

Sometimes there's a subtle longing for it.

To be alone in my own silence.

Perfume

I wonder what her perfume smells like.

If it lingers on her skin, strong or faint.

Gardenias are the scent she wears,

I want to smell it in the air.

I could buy a bottle to quell my curiosity

But I would rather wait till the day I get to hug her.

To learn that smell.

And when that day comes, I will hold onto it.

Hold onto her and the smell that comes with her.

Crystal Clear

I used to feel like a book with no ending.

Like a song with no final chord.

But then you came along, making me laugh and smile,

and somehow, just like that,

I got all involved.

You speak to me like a poem I wrote in another life.

I always breathe a bit slower when you say goodnight.

Maybe the stars knew long before we did.

Some souls are drawn where the rest always hide.

You don't have to try, you just understand me.

Like my heart had been holding out for the beat of yours.

We've got the same dreams and the same kind of fears.

We see each other crystal clear.

Found

You write about hope in a world full of ache.

I'd read every sentence, no matter how late.

And if this life is a map with no guide,

I'd still follow you blind through the dark every time.

Not because I'm lost, but because I've been found

in the quiet between us.

Spilt Milk

How often have I cried over spilled milk?

It would never cry over me.

I sob and sniffle and wipe my blurry eyes.

Wiping up the milk, shoulders hunched in

hiccuping as I take in shaky breaths.

Watching it pool like a small,

white apology I wasn't ready to accept.

Conversations With The Wind

A gentle breeze flows around me.

Swaying side to side.

As it breathes out soft words.

Carries like a melody.

A comforting song, as it speaks to me.

I tell the wind I missed it.

That I looked for it every time I turned a corner.

Waiting for its kind touch to be my solace in the Florida heat.

Web

Time is not a line,

It's a web.

Interconnecting points spiraling around each other.

Winding around and around.

Bringing you to different events

then back to the same ones again & again.

Colorful Again

The world has slowly gained color again.

The grass and trees are green.

The sky is bright blue.

No more dull and sad colors,

the world no longer looks so bland.

Color is bleeding back into everything again.

And the world is starting to look like the world again.

Go

I've gotten good at letting go.

Detaching myself before I get hurt,

because I have been hurt one too many times.

Sometimes I let go before I should.

Dealing the damage to myself before it's truly time.

The Day Everything Almost Changed

I will never forget that notification.

7:07 pm

A cry for my mom ripped my throat.

Fear and tears was all I could feel in a matter of seconds.

Rushing.Driving. Praying.

For his life to be safe.

The Trees Knew First

The trees knew before we did.

Long before, they felt the shift in the air.

The sun is growing harsher.

The natural elements are meaner.

Their soil started lacking in nutrients.

And their brothers and sisters began to dwindle.

They feel the harsh truth,

before many came to terms with it.

Humans have turned destructive.

Scaring and harming the earth.

Taking and taking until forests turned empty

and the sun burned too hot on us.

The trees knew first.

What kind of world are we turning everything into?

The trees feel the pain as our one and only planet is hurt and abused.

And it will continue to feel that hurt for years to come.

How To Unlove Someone (In Steps)

Step One

Cry until you can't any more.

Mourn the loss of the present and what the future could have been.

Step Two

Shuffle through days while everything feels gray.

You feel like your life is over (It's not, you just don't realize that yet.)

Step Three

Slowly accept your new reality.

Let life pick up pace again as you put yourself back together.

Step Four

Move on, life doesn't halt forever,

It will keep moving whether you want it to or not, grow with it.

I Used To Be A Storm, Now I'm The Sea

I used to be angry.

So angry it would roll off in waves.

Tsunamis of sadness and rage.

Swarming the beaches and taking over everything.

Dark clouds are hovering over everything.

Darkening whatever is in its reach.

And it was like that for a while.

Storm after storm.

Rough wave after rough wave.

Hitting the seashore.

Then one day it stopped.

The sea calmed, and the clouds cleared.

The waves turned gentle and kind.

The air no longer charged with a thick kind of hatred.

The sky lightened, and the waves swayed.

No longer so angry as it passed its days.

Me?

I am not who I was,

but I am still me.

When I look at old pictures,

I do not recognize the person looking back at me.

It is me, yes.

But not.

I am no longer the person in that photo.

I've experienced more life and things

they hadn't even started to imagine.

I've seen more,

felt deeper,

and learned to be gentle

with the parts

that once made me small.

I'm older, wiser

and still becoming

a reflection that keeps shifting,

but never disappears.

You Only Call Me When It Rains

I'm never surprised,

when the weather turns gray.

I know you'll call out my name.

I wait for my phone to ring.

Wait for your call to display.

When I answer, you always say

'It's raining today,

It made me think of you'

And think of me, you did.

You always call when it rains.

Say it was such a pretty day.

Saying the rain made it such a pretty day.

Overthink

How is it that one word can cause me to overthink?

If a message just sounds slightly odd,

now I'm wondering if you even want to talk to me at all.

I'm sure it's not that deep,

but still, I'm overthinking anything you've ever said to me.

The Sun Apologized Today

The sun apologized today.

It came in the morning, leaving soft kisses on my face.

It whispered that it was sorry,

for being gone so long.

Lingering near to let me know it's there.

It told me it will stay for a while.

Keep away the cold and

Rainy weather for just a little longer.

Just for me, so I could feel its embrace.

Words You Find Dear

Sometimes words escape me.

I know what I want to say,

but the words don't make it out.

I fear too much for other people's feelings.

Silencing my thoughts and filtering my words.

In hopes to keep any disturbance from slipping in.

Childish, I know.

But the fear of upsetting you lingers,

so I suppress myself.

And only mutter words you find dear.

Ache

When I see your face, it gives me a bellyache.

You're such a disgrace.

A Muse, A Poet

I find you in everything beautiful.

Even when I try not to,

you are there.

I have conditioned myself to see you always.

In every ray of sunlight.

In every speck of glitter.

In every paint stroke.

Your hair. Your eyes.

Your smile. Your light.

I think everything worthwhile

was created with you in mind.

My muse.

Envy

The moon watches the horizon ignite,

a coin of pale silver.

outshone by a furnace of gold.

She drifts in silence,

draped in borrowed light,

Knowing her glow,

is nothing more than a reflection.

A secret she hides behind craters

and shadows.

The sun blazes,

worshiped by fields,

mirrored in oceans.

Sung about in the voices of morning.

And the moon,

with her quiet pull on tides and hearts,

wonders why whispers

never carry as far as songs.

She envies the applause of daylight.

The warmth that ripens fruit

and paints the earth in color.

Yet when night falls,

and lovers lift their faces to her

and poets spill ink in her name,

she remembers.

Envy cannot dim her.

Even reflected light

is enough

to make the darkness listen.

Comfort

Steam curls like gentle fingers,

reaching upward,

brushing the edge of a tired face.

The cup rests warm in weary hands,

Its porcelain heartbeat steady,

whispering stay.

Just for a moment.

Leaves steep their quiet wisdom.

Releasing amber comfort

that tastes of patience,

of earth, of time unhurried.

Each sip softens the edges.

The ache behind the eyes,

the weight pressed into the chest.

The tea does not demand healing:

It only offers presence.

A small, steady kindness,

a hush in the storm.

And for a breath,

the soul unclenches.

Not fixed,

but soothed,

like a child rocked

in the arms of something safe.

No Sound Remains

The air hangs thick,

not with words,

but with the absence of them.

The room remembers the echoes.

Sharp syllables flung like stones,

promises cracked at the edges.

Now nothing stirs

but the hum of a clock

that dares to keep moving forward.

Two mouths stay closed,

as if silence might stitch

what speech has torn.

But the quiet is not gentle:

It presses,

dense as smoke,

settling into lungs.

Eyes turn away.

Hands twitch for something to hold

but find only the cold.

Divided between chair and chairs.

It is silence that tastes of ash,

that asks without asking:

Was the truth spoken?

Or only the hurt?

And though no sound remains,

the argument lives on

a shadow neither one can name,

but both can feel curling in the corners of the room.

Bleeding

If time heals,

why do some wounds keep

bleeding years later?

Dripping, dripping down

leaving a quiet trail of silenced

pain in its wake.

The Moon Listens

Does the moon ever tire?

Tire from carrying our secrets at night?

Listening to our whispered fears

and our hushed woes.

Always lending an ear

being a silver pillar for us to feel.

Surrender

The forest has surrendered.

Its branches raised in quiet resignation,

each tree stripped down to bone.

But one remains unwilling.

It grips a single leaf,

like a memory clenched in a dying hand.

The seasons circle,

cold sharpening its breath,

yet the stem refuses release.

Is it pride that binds it?

Or love?

Maybe an old devotion to what once was?

Perhaps grief,

the kind that cannot imagine

becoming anything else.

The leaf trembles in the wind,

a fragile heart on display,

Its veins darkening,

Its body whispers of the soil's embrace.

Still, it lingers,

a prayer against inevitability,

a question pressed into silence.

If letting go is the way of all things,

why does holding on

sometimes feel more sacred?

Longing

The ache settles deep in my chest when I think of you

Your face appears behind my eyes.

A person I never met,

I genuinely get upset because

our paths might not cross.

I try to think of others, but my thoughts return to you.

What am I supposed to do?

My heartburns when I see your face.

Is it the same for you?

Or am I alone in the longing I have for you?

Skin Of Stars

The night stretches wide,

a dark skin stitched with light.

Each star a wound.

Long since closed,

a memory of fire

that burned itself away.

We gaze upward

and call it beautiful,

never asking what pain

was torn into the fabric first.

Galaxies bloom like bruises,

constellations trace the shapes

of healed violence.

Forgotten wars.

Collapsed suns.

Perhaps the sky is not infinite.

Perhaps it is only

the body of something ancient.

Marked by all it has endured.

And when we wish on stars,

we are whispering our hopes

into scars

that once carried

someone else's sorrow.

Safety In The Rain

The sky begins to hum,

a gentle tapping at the glass.

Not thunder,

not a storm.

Only a rhythm

meant to quiet restless hearts.

Each note is a drop,

falling into place,

a melody stitched together by water and air.

It does not rush.

It does not demand.

It simply lingers,

a hush spread wide across the night.

The roof becomes a cradle,

the windows a drum,

And in that steady chorus

the world feels smaller,

softer,

safe.

Rain sings the language of sleep,

and in its arms

even sorrow

learns how to close its eyes.

My Stone Of Lonely

Loneliness is a stone.

I keep it in my pocket,

cold against my palm,

heavy though it fits

in the smallest space.

I take it out sometimes,

turn it over in my hand.

Trace the grooves,

where the others have held their own.

It doesn't speak,

but it presses.

Reminding me it's there,

shaping the curve of my grip.

I could throw it,

leave it in the dirt.

But somehow

I always slip it back

into my pocket.

Because it is familiar.

Because it belongs to me.

Because even weight

is a kind of company.

It Remembers Everything

The river does not forget.

It carries more than water.

It carries the weight of what has

passed through it.

Pebbles smoothed to silence.

Branches broken, drifting.

Ash from fires no one speaks of.

Names whispered into its current

like confessions.

Children once skipped stones here,

their laughter sinking into it.

Lovers carved initials on its banks,

their promises washed downstream

tears folded into its body.

Never returned.

And though it moves,

always forward.

It is never empty.

Memory clings to its depths,

coiling around reeds and rocks,

singing in the undertow.

Stand beside it long enough,

and you will hear them.

All the voices,

all the fragments,

woven into one endless story

the river refuses to release.

Symphony Of Thunder

First, the violins.

A hush of rain,

soft strings plucking

against windows and leaves.

Then the drums roll

thunder swelling in the distance,

a low and patient thrum

summoning the dark.

Flutes join in,

the whistle of the wind

threading through branches,

a melody rising and bending.

The brass arrives

Lightning, sudden and fierce,

a trumpet's cry

splitting the sky wide open.

The conductor is unseen,

yet every note obeys.

Crescendo in fury,

pause in silence.

Then the final chord.

A downpour,

wild and relentless.

Until at last,

the music softens,

lingers,

and fades.

A Conversation Between The Mountain & Wind

The mountain said to the wind,

"Why do you rush so endlessly?

I have stood for centuries,

Yet you never stop moving."

The wind laughed softly, brushing

snow from the peak.

"Because I must carry the voices you

are too heavy to hold.

The cries of oceans,

the whispers of trees.

The secrets men let slip in the dark."

The mountain rumbled low,

stones shifting in its chest.

"And yet, when you leave. I remain.

I hold silence the way you hold sound."

The wind circled once more,

curling into the mountain's ear.

"True, but even silence erodes,

and even the stone remembers me.

Every curve of your body,

every scar on your face.

They are proof

that I was here."

And so they spoke.

One restless. One rooted.

Forever, different.

Forever bound.

It Waits For Them To Come Home

The house inhales at dusk,

drawing shadows through broken shutters.

Exhaling dust into empty rooms.

No footsteps mark the floorboards now,

yet they creak.

Complaining softly to themselves,

remembering the weight that will not return.

The fireplace sighs.

Though no fire warms it.

The windows fog,

though no hands press against the glass.

Neighbors swear it listens.

That if you linger by the porch

you can hear a pulse in the rafters.

A quiet heart,

that never learned

how to stop.

Perhaps it waits.

Not for the living,

but for the one who left.

A breath held too long,

a chest that will not empty

until its master comes home.

What Will You Think Of Me

I can only wonder what you think of me?

If you get a clear image through my deflection.

My words flow freely to you

can you hear my pain?

Or did my pretty words distract you from

what I really mean?

All my thoughts cloud my head.

Too many to get through,

so many slipping between the cracks.

I wonder how you ever see through that.

You say you see me,

but I know it isn't true.

You see what I want you to see.

Maybe it's the other way around,

who am I to disagree?

If I were to abandon the facade

would you recognize me?

Or would my true ways scare you

and make you think I'm beyond being

saved?

Would you flinch when the mask scatters to

the floor?

When you find out the reasons why I don't

sleep.

I wonder if you'll close me up like you never

peeked.

Or if you'll leave me gaping and half empty

once you decide to leave.

Tell me what you want to see.

Tell me who I should be.

Because who I really am, you simply

wouldn't understand.

The Moon And Her Love For The Ocean

Each night,

the moon dips her pen in silver light

and writes across the waves.

Her letters drift folded in reflections,

sealed in longing.

She tells the ocean

how she misses the way it shimmered

when they were young together,

when tides rose eagerly just to touch her glow.

Now, the sea only murmurs,

busy with storms and ships,

with secrets and salt.

It takes her words

and pulls them under,

never sending an answer back.

Still, she writes.

Every night.

Because hope,

like the tide,

is a rhythm she cannot unlearn.

And when dawn comes,

she fades.

Ink spent.

Heart emptied.

Trusting that somewhere,

beneath all that blue silence

the ocean is still reading.

Sunlight

It begins softly.

A hush of gold slipping through the half closed curtains,

as if the light itself

is afraid to wake the silence.

Dust turns to constellations,

floating in the air like slow music.

The floor glows,

the chairs hum with quiet warmth.

And the walls,

once gray with sleep,

remember color again.

The morning light does not rush.

It lingers on forgotten corners,

on the rim of a teacup,

on the spine of a book left half-read.

It touches everything.

As if it forgives it.

And in that moment,

before the day begins, it's noise,

the whole room breathes.

Alive.

Golden.

Forgiven.

New.

Unlikely Odds

Something blooms in an unlikely place.

Green weaving through cement

trying and trying to find a place

and finally has a breakthrough.

Reaching the sun and stretching high.

Bulbs form and flowers bloom.

Something delicate in a place that had no room.

The hustle and bustle of the street

doesn't stop for the flower.

Life is too busy for that

but no one disrupts it either

leaving it be.

Some passersby appreciating.

The small beauty in a world

full of machines and gloom.

Many wondering how something

like that could bloom.

Change

A year from now,

I like to think

that I will be far away from here.

In a place I've only dreamed of.

With new places and faces.

Living the life I so desperately want to lead.

Chasing education and career,

new friends that will be real.

Living a happy life in

a country I don't fear.

One day, I will move away and

run to everything I want.

And everyone I cherish will do their things.

None of us will be the same.

That is something I pray for every single day.

Can't Worry About It

I don't talk about it,

I don't have the time.

To dwell on things I can't control.

People, politics, fear, sadness.

I don't bother talking about things I can't decide.

My Friends

I don't remember much from then.

Just the heartache and confusion.

I remember I was lonely.

I don't know what I wanted

I just wanted to be heard.

And to keep my friends.

Revisions

Every time you open the page,

the words shift.

Quietly, as if ashamed

of what they said before.

Yesterday, it was about love.

Soft, forgiving, golden.

Today, it's about loss,

and the ache that hides beneath every sunrise.

The lines rearrange themselves.

Like a restless soul,

never sure which truth fits best.

A comma becomes a wound,

a period, a prayer.

Perhaps it's not the poem that changes.

But you.

The one who reads,

the one who carries new scars.

And softer hands each time you return.

So the poem learns you,

rewrites itself to fit your shape,

bends its ink to your breathing.

Until one day,

you find it blank.

As if it has given all its words away,

and now waits.

Quietly,

for you to write the rest.

The Lullaby Beneath The Leaves

At night, the forest hums.

Not loud enough to wake the stars,

but enough that the wind pauses to listen.

The trees breathe in unison,

their roots tangled like veins

beneath the skin of the Earth.

Each leaf trembles

with the echo of an old lullaby.

A song older than rain,

older than language.

The soil murmurs secrets

to the sleeping seeds, promising them dawn.

A fox curls beneath a fern,

Its heartbreak syncing to the rhythm of roots.

If you stand still long enough,

you can hear it

the low hymn of everything that grows,

of life that never truly rests.

And in that soft, endless hum,

you realize

even in stillness,

the world keeps singing.

The Sunset Wouldn't Leave

It stayed longer than it should have.

Spilling gold across the rooftops,

bleeding lights into the horizon

like a promise that didn't know how to end.

The sky blushed,

then hesitated,

Its color clinging to the edges of clouds

like fingertips on a closing door.

Even the wind grew still,

afraid to hurry the moment.

The day held its breath,

and the world seemed caught

between goodbye and not yet.

Perhaps the sun, too,

knows what it means to linger.

To ache for what it must leave behind

to set, but not want to.

And so it burned a little longer,

a last flare of wanting

before surrendering to the dark.

The Messenger

A crow lifts from the fencepost,

black feathers catching the dull light

of a half-hearted morning.

In its beak, a ribbon,

frayed and thin,

the color of old rain.

It flies low,

skimming over fields

where the frost still remembers footsteps,

towards another waiting shadow

perched on the rusted gate.

They do not caw,

do not bow,

do not blink,

one passes the ribbon to the other.

A silent exchange,

a secret too heavy for language.

Maybe it's a gift.

Maybe it's a warning.

Maybe it's simply what crows do.

Carry what we leave behind,

piece by piece,

to places we'll never reach.

And when both vanish into the treeline,

the morning falls lighter,

as if some small sorrow

has finally been delivered.

What I Can't Hear Anymore

It doesn't vanish all at once.

It slips away in echoes

a note held too long,

then gone before you notice.

First, the laughter dulls,

edges blurring like a song

played from another room.

Then the words begin to lose their shape,

syllables falling through the cracks of time.

You try to hold the sound.

Press it to your ear

like a seashell from a distant shore

but even the ocean forgets its own waves.

Soon, it's only the rhythm that remains,

a heartbeat that once matches yours.

Then silence

soft,

merifcul,

like snow covering everything

you once could name.

And you realize,

some things don't disappear.

They just learn

to live quietly

in the spaces

where they once were heard.

Doors

In a hallway of dreams and half

remembered days,

there is a door that waits.

Old brass handle, wood worn smooth

by every hand you've ever had.

When you open it,

you don't step forward.

You unravel.

Behind it:

A thousand rooms,

each lit by a different version of your

laughter.

One of you never left home.

One still believes in miracles.

One wears grief like a coat that finally fits.

You watch them move.

Their gestures almost yours.

Their eyes almost know you.

Some glance up, startled,

as if sensing the shadow

of another life peering in.

You want to ask them.

You have so many questions.

Which of us got it right?

Which of us found peace?

But the words catch on the threshold.

Because the truth hums softly.

In the hinges and floorboards.

Every door you open leads to another you still becoming.

And so you close it.

Not in fear.

But in reverence.

Some mirrors are too wide

for one lifetime to cross.

Smaller And Lighter

One morning

I reached for it.

The familiar heaviness

that used to wait beside my bed

and found only light.

It startled me,

how silence could feel so kind,

how breathing didn't ache

the way it used to.

For so long,

I carried sorrow like a second skin,

believing it was part of who I was.

That to lose it would mean losing myself.

But now,

when I look back,

it feels smaller,

like a childhood coat

I can no longer fit inside.

It still hangs somewhere

in the closet of memory,

stitched with all I've survived.

But I don't wear it anymore.

And that,

I think,

Is what healing truly is.

Not forgetting the rain.

But learning.

How to walk beneath the sun

without flinching.

The Sound Of Forgiveness

It isn't loud.

Not the shatter of glass,

not the thunder of release.

It's softer.

A sound you almost miss

If you're still listening for pain.

It begins as a sigh,

a loosening in the chest,

like a door finally unlatched after years of rust.

It sounds like footsteps.

Leaving without bitterness,

like rain falling on something once scorched.

It hums beneath the ribs,

gentle as breath after crying,

as if the heart is learning its language again.

Forgiveness doesn't announce itself.

It arrives quietly,

sits beside you in silence,

and teaches you how to hear peace.

Dimmer

Tonight, the sky feels heavier.

A vast, black canvas

threadbare in places

where light used to live.

It wears its emptiness

like grief too deep for sound,

stretching endlessly but never whole.

The wind passes through,

carrying whispers of what once shone.

Name forgotten,

fires gone out quietly,

as if tired of being wished upon.

The moon tries to comfort,

but even she flickers,

her glow dimmed by the weight of remembering.

Somewhere,

a star is being born

but the sky still weeps

for the ones it's lost.

The ones that burned too bright,

too fast, and left silence

where brilliance used to be.

And maybe that's all mourning is.

Loving the light long after it's gone.

And still looking up,

just incase something decides

to return.

What The Light Left Behind

Morning doesn't rush anymore.

It spills softly through the curtains,

like it knows I'm still learning

how to meet the day.

Dust floats through gold,

and for a moment,

the room feels like a place

the world forgot to hurry.

There are coffee rings

on the table,

pages half-turned,

a quiet hum

of something unfinished.

But breathing.

And maybe that's enough:

to be here,

not as who I was,

or who I should be,

but simply as someone

the light still finds.

What We Leave Behind

There are ghosts in the small things,

a sweater still holding its shape,

a teacup with a chipped rim,

the dent in a pillow

that never quite flattens out.

I find them when I'm not looking,

in the hush between tasks,

in the way dust gathers on the edge

of something once loved.

Time moves like water,

quiet and certain,

smoothing every sharp edge

I swore I'd never lose.

And yet, somewhere beneath it all,

I remain in everything,

a whisper of laughter in an empty room,

a fingerprint on a windowpane,

proof that even the smallest moments

refuse to fade completely.

Becoming

There was a time,

when I mistook noise for living.

When I chased every spark

just to prove I could burn.

I called rest a weakness,

mistook stillness for loss,

and filled the silence

with anything that glittered

enough to distract me from myself.

But slowly,

the fire softened.

I learned that not every ending

means failure.

That not every silence

is empty.

Peace came quietly.

Not as triumph,

but as understanding.

It taught me to listen

instead of win.

To forgive instead of forget.

Now, the storms still come,

but I no longer beg them to stop.

I open the window,

let the rain fall where it must,

and trust,

that what's meant to bloom

will find its way

through the mud.

About The Author

From the moment she learned to read as a toddler, storytelling became her world. As a young child, she crafted handmade books for friends and family, laying the foundation for a lifelong love of words. By adolescence, she had spent countless hours immersed in reading, sharpening the voice that would soon emerge in her own writing.

At just 14, she was published under a pen name, and by 15, she had completed her debut novella. By 16, she released her first poetry collection along with a set of writing guides designed to support and inspire budding authors. These works further cemented her role not only as a creator but also as a mentor to other young writers finding their voices. Graduating high school early, she continued to break barriers, becoming—before the age of 18—a cofounder and Head of the Teen Author Division at Luminary Publishing House.

Her journey reflects not only precocious talent but also a deep commitment to empowering young voices in literature.